QUINTET

for Guitar and String Quartet
in A major, Opus 65

Introduction
GRAVE

Guitar

Andantino
THEME

Mauro Giuliani
Opus 65

3

Guitar

4

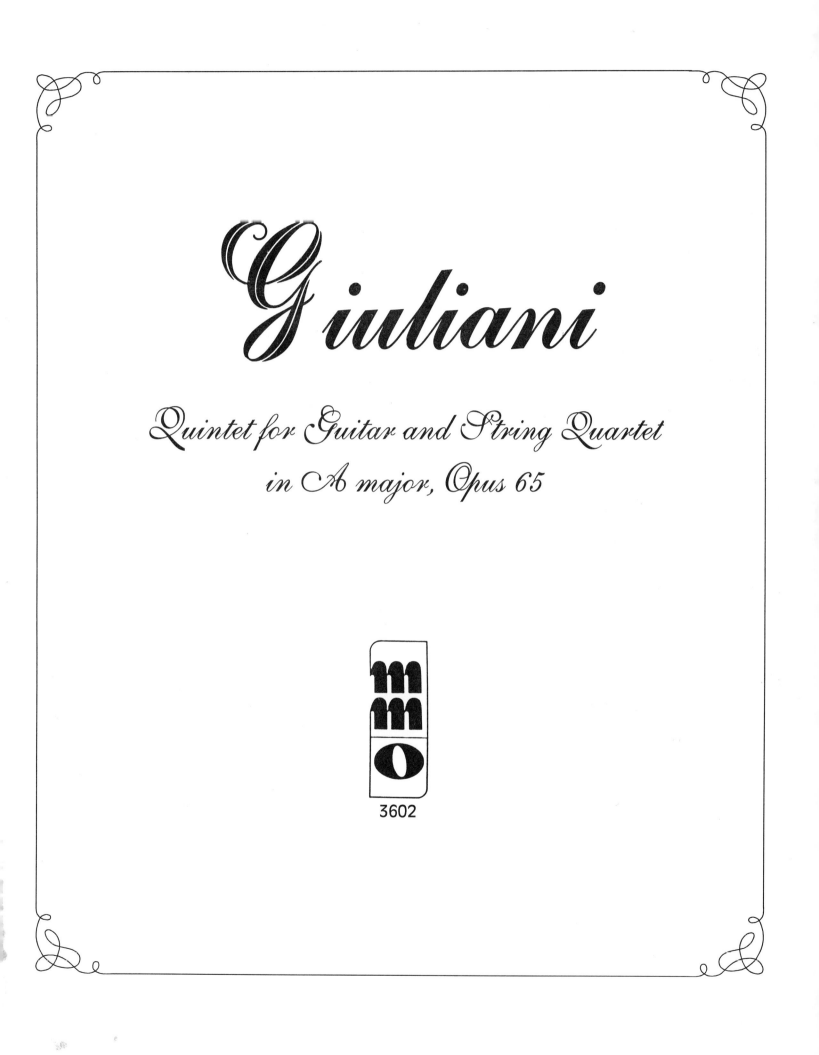

Giuliani

Quintet for Guitar and String Quartet
in A major, Opus 65

3602

COMPACT DISC BAND AND PAGE INFORMATION

MMO CD 3602

Music Minus One

MAURO
GUILIANI
Guitar Quintet in A Major, Opus 65

Andante sostenuto

tap tap tap tap tap

Solo

Variation 4

9

Guitar

10

Guitar

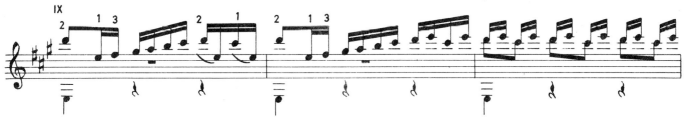

Guitar

12

Guitar

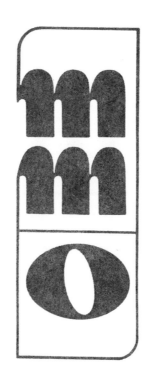

MUSIC MINUS ONE COMPACT DISC CATALOG

Music Minus One PIANO Compact Discs

MMO CD 3001 Beethoven Piano Concerto No. 1 in C, Opus 15
*MMO CD 3002 Beethoven Piano Concerto No. 2 in Bb, Opus 19
MMO CD 3003 Beethoven Piano Concerto No. 3 in Cm, Opus 37
*MMO CD 3004 Beethoven Piano Concerto No. 4 in G, Opus 58
*MMO CD 3005 Beethoven Piano Concerto No. 5 in Eb, Opus 73
MMO CD 3006 Grieg Piano Concerto in A minor, Opus 16
MMO CD 3007 Rachmaninoff Piano Concerto No. 2 in C minor
*MMO CD 3008 Schumann Piano Concerto in A minor, Opus 54
*MMO CD 3009 Brahms Piano Concerto No. 1 in D minor, Opus 15
MMO CD 3010 Chopin Piano Concerto No. 1 in Em, Opus 11
*MMO CD 3011 Mendelssohn Piano Concerto No. 1 in Gm, Opus 25
MMO CD 3012 W.A. Mozart Piano Concerto No. 9 in Ebm, K.271
MMO CD 3013 W.A. Mozart Piano Concerto No. 12 in A, K.414
*MMO CD 3014 W.A. Mozart Piano Concerto No. 20 in Dm, K.466
MMO CD 3015 W.A. Mozart Piano Concerto No. 23 in A, K.488
MMO CD 3016 W.A. Mozart Piano Concerto No. 24 in Cm, K.491
*MMO CD 3017 W.A. Mozart Piano Concerto No. 26 in D, 'Coronation'
MMO CD 3018 W.A. Mozart Piano Concerto in G major, K.453
*MMO CD 3019 Liszt Piano Concerto No. 1/Weber Concertstucke
*MMO CD 3020 Liszt Piano Concerto No. 2/Hungarian Fantasia
MMO CD 3021 J.S. Bach Piano Concerto in Fm/J.C. Bach Concerto in Eb
MMO CD 3022 J.S. Bach Piano Concerto in D minor
MMO CD 3023 Haydn Piano Concerto in D major
*MMO CD 3024 Heart Of The Piano Concerto
*MMO CD 3025 Themes From The Great Piano Concerti
MMO CD 3026 Tschiakowsky Piano Concerto No. 1 in Bbm, Opus 23
*Available Winter 1994/Spring 1995

Music Minus One VOCALIST Compact Discs

MMO CD 4001 Schubert Lieder for High Voice
MMO CD 4002 Schubert Lieder for Low Voice
MMO CD 4003 Schubert Lieder for High Voice   volume 2
MMO CD 4004 Schubert Lieder for Low Voice   volume 2
MMO CD 4005 Brahms Lieder for High Voice
MMO CD 4006 Brahms Lieder for Low Voice
MMO CD 4007 Everybody's Favorite Songs for High Voice
MMO CD 4008 Everybody's Favorite Songs for Low Voice
MMO CD 4009 Everybody's Favorite Songs for High Voice   volume 2
MMO CD 4010 Everybody's Favorite Songs for Low Voice   volume 2
MMO CD 4011 17th/18th Century Italian Songs High Voice
MMO CD 4012 17th/18th Century Italian Songs Low Voice
MMO CD 4013 17th/18th Century Italian Songs High Voice   volume 2
MMO CD 4014 17th/18th Century Italian Songs Low Voice   volume 2
MMO CD 4015 Famous Soprano Arias
MMO CD 4016 Famous Mezzo-Soprano Arias
MMO CD 4017 Famous Tenor Arias
MMO CD 4018 Famous Bratione Arias
MMO CD 4019 Famous Bass Arias
MMO CD 4020 Hugo Wolf Lieder for High Voice
MMO CD 4021 Hugo Wolf Lieder for Low Voice
MMO CD 4022 Richard Strauss Lieder for High Voice
MMO CD 4023 Richard Strauss Lieder for Low Voice
MMO CD 4024 Robert Schumann Lieder for High Voice
MMO CD 4025 Robert Schumann Lieder for Low Voice
MMO CD 4026 W.A. Mozart Arias For Soprano
MMO CD 4027 Verdi Arias For Soprano
MMO CD 4028 Italian Arais For Soprano
MMO CD 4029 French Arias For Soprano
MMO CD 4030 Soprano Oratorio Arias
MMO CD 4031 Alto Oratorio Arias
MMO CD 4032 Tenor Oratorio Arias
MMO CD 4033 Bass Oratorio Arias
John Wustman, Piano Accompanist

Music Minus One CLARINET Compact Discs

*MMO CD 3201 Mozart Clarinet Concerto in A major
*MMO CD 3202 Weber Clarinet Concerto No. 1 in F minor, Op. 73
          Stamitz Clarinet Concerto No. 3 in Bb major
*MMO CD 3203 Spohr Clarinet Concerto No. 1 in C minor, Op. 26
*MMO CD 3204 Weber Clarinet Concertino, Opus 26
MMO CD 3205 First Chair Clarinet Solos *Orchestral Excerpts*
MMO CD 3206 The Art Of The Solo Clarinet *Orchestral Excerpts*
*MMO CD 3207 Mozart: Quintet of Clarinet and Strings in A, K.581
*MMO CD 3208 Brahms: Sonatas Opus 120, Nos. 1 & 2
*MMO CD 3209 Weber: Grand Duo Concertant - Wagner: Adagio
*MMO CD 3210 Schumann Fantasy Pieces, Opus 73, Three Romances
MMO CD 3211 Easy Clarinet Solos, Student Editions 1-3 years
MMO CD 3212 Easy Clarinet Solos, Student Editions 1-3 years, vol. 2
*Available Spring 1995

Music Minus One TRUMPET Compact Discs

*MMO CD 3801 Haydn: Eb; Telemann D major; Fasch D major Concerto
*MMO CD 3802 Easy Trumpet Solos, Student Editions 1-3 years
*MMO CD 3803 Easy Trumpet Solos, Student Editions 1-3 years, vol. 2

Music Minus One VIOLIN Compact Discs

MMO CD 3100 Bruch Violin Concerto in Gm
MMO CD 3101 Mendelssohn Violin Concerto in Em
MMO CD 3102 Tschaikovsky Violin Concerto in D, Opus 35
MMO CD 3103 J.S. Bach "Double" Concerto in Dm
MMO CD 3104 J.S. Bach Violin Concerti in Am/E
MMO CD 3105 J.S. Bach Brandenburg Concerti Nos. 4 and 5
MMO CD 3106 J.S. Bach Brandenburg No. 2/Triple Concerto
MMO CD 3107 J.S. Bach Concerto in Dm
*MMO CD 3108 Brahms Violin Concerto in D, Opus 77
*MMO CD 3109 Chausson Poeme/Schubert Rondo
MMO CD 3110 Lalo Symphonie Espagnole
MMO CD 3111 Mozart Concerto in D/Vivaldi Concerto in Am
MMO CD 3112 Mozart Violin Concerto in A, K.219
MMO CD 3113 Wieniawski Concerto in D/Sarasate Zigeunerweisen
MMO CD 3114 Viotti Concerto No. 22
MMO CD 3115 Beethoven Two Romances/"Spring" Sonata
MMO CD 3116 St. Saëns Intro & Rondo Cap./Mozart Serenade & Adagio
MMO CD 3117 Beethoven Violin Concerto in D major, Opus 61
MMO CD 3118 The Concertmaster Solos from Symphonic Works
MMO CD 3119 Air On A G String Favorite Encores for Orchestra
MMO CD 3120 Concert Pieces For The Serious Violinist
MMO CD 3121 Eighteenth Century Violin Music
MMO CD 3122 Violin Favorites With Orchestra Vol. 1 (Easy)
MMO CD 3123 Violin Favorites With Orchestra Vol. 2 (Moderate)
MMO CD 3124 Violin Favorites With Orchestra Vol. 3 (Mod. Diff.)
MMO CD 3125 The Three B's: Bach/Beethoven/Brahms
MMO CD 3126 Vivaldi Concerti in Am, D, Am Opus 3 No. 6,9,8
MMO CD 3127 Vivaldi "The Four Seasons" 2 CD set $29.98 each
MMO CD 3128 Vivaldi "La Tempesta di Mare" Opus 8 No. 5
          Albinoni: Violin Concerto in A
MMO CD 3129 Vivaldi: Violin Concerto Opus 3 No. 12
*Spring 1995   Vivaldi Violin Concerto Opus 8, No. 6 "Il Piacere"

Music Minus One FLUTE Compact Discs

MMO CD 3300 Mozart Concerto in D/Quantz Concerto in G
MMO CD 3301 Mozart Flute Concerto in G major
MMO CD 3302 J.S. Bach Suite No. 2 in Bm
MMO CD 3303 Boccherini/Vivaldi Concerti/Mozart Andante
MMO CD 3304 Haydn/Vivaldi/Frederick "The Great" Concerti
MMO CD 3305 Vivaldi/Telemann/Leclair Flute Concerti
MMO CD 3306 J.S. Bach Brandenburg No. 2/Haydn Concerto
MMO CD 3307 J.S. Bach Triple Concerto/Vivaldi Concerto No. 9
*MMO CD 3308 Mozart/Stamitz Flute Quartets
*MMO CD 3309 Haydn London Trios
*MMO CD 3310 J.S. Bach Brandenburg Concerti No. 4 and No. 5
*MMO CD 3311 W.A. Mozart Three Flute Quartets
*MMO CD 3312 Telemann Am Suite/Gluck 'Orpheus' Scene/Pergolesi Conc. in G
*MMO CD 3313 Flute Song Easy familiar Classics
MMO CD 3314 Vivaldi 3 Flute Concerti RV 427, 438, Opus 10 No. 5
MMO CD 3315 Vivaldi 3 Flute Concerti RV 440, Opus 10 No. 4, RV 429
MMO CD 3316 Easy Flute Solos, Student Editions 1-3 years
MMO CD 3317 Easy Flute Solos, Student Editions 1-3 years, vol. 2
*Fall 1994

Music Minus One OBOE Compact Discs

MMO CD 3400 Albinoni Three Oboe Concerti Opus 7 No. 3, No. 6, Opus 9 No. 2
MMO CD 3401 3 Oboe Concerti: Handel, Telemann, Vivaldi
MMO CD 3402 Mozart/Stamitz Oboe Quartets in F major (K.370; Op.8 #3)

Music Minus One FRENCH HORN Compact Discs

*MMO CD 3501 Mozart: Concerto No. 2, K.417; No. 3, K.447
*Spring 1995

Music Minus One GUITAR Compact Discs

MMO CD 3601 Boccherini: Guitar Quintet, No. 4 in D major
MMO CD 3602 Giuliani: Guitar Quintet, Opus 65

Music Minus One CELLO Compact Discs

*MMO CD 3701 Dvorak: Cello Concerto in B minor, Opus 104
*MMO CD 3702 C.P.E. Bach: Cello Concerto in A minor
*MMO CD 3703 Boccherini: Concerto in Bb Major; Bruch: Kol Nidrei
*Spring 1995

Music Minus One TROMBONE Compact Discs

MMO CD 3901 Easy Trombone Solos, Student Editions 1-3 years
MMO CD 3902 Easy Trombone Solos, Student Editions 1-3 years, vol. 2

Music Minus One ALTO SAX Compact Discs

*MMO CD 4101 Easy Alto Sax Solos, Student Editions 1-3 years
*MMO CD 4102 Easy Alto Sax Solos, Student Editions 1-3 years, vol. 2

MUSIC MINUS ONE • 50 Executive Boulevard • Elmsford, New York 10523-1325 • Phone: 914-592-1188 • Fax: 914-592-3116